PERSONAL FINANCE AND MONEY

Toye Adelaja

ISBN (978 1517030810)

INTRODUCTION

Personal finance is the whole processes involved in earning income, receiving gifts, saving money and spending money. Personal finance is very vital to every human's existence. It is like a blood flowing through the veins of human beings, and hence it should be handled with care and prominence it deserves.

TABLE OF CONTENTS

CHAPTER ONE

INTRODUCTION TO PERSONAL FINANCE

1.1. Personal Finance

Personal finance is the whole processes involved in earning income, receiving gifts, saving money and spending money. Personal finance is very vital to every human's existence. It is like a blood flowing through the veins of human beings, and hence it should be handled with care and prominence it deserves.

As business finance is important to every business so is personal finance is important to every human. If a business is well financed, the business will be flourishing. If a person is well financed, the person will be well and have a bright future. Every business transaction is recorded on daily basis. The same thing should be applied to personal transaction. Personal transaction such as receiving of income, savings and spending of money should be recorded on daily basis.

Business entity borrows money to execute projects. The entity manages the loan and ensures that the loan is paid with interest as at when due. Human beings can also obtain loan and ensure that the loan is paid with interest as at when due.

1.2. Record Keeping

Record keeping is a pivotal element of personal finance. Record keeping is the methods of recoding every transaction involved in personal finance. It ranges from recording of salary or any other income received, recording of savings and recording of any money spent. Record keeping could be cumbersome to some people and it can be simple to some people. It depends on the way you perceive and practice it. Some people record every cent of their transaction while some ignore immaterial transaction.

It is advisable to record every transaction irrespective of the amount involved.

1.2.1. Reasons for Record Keeping

The following are the reasons for record keeping:

1) **To know where your income is coming from and to track it**

Recording of your income enables you to know the source or sources of your income. It enables you to know whether you have received all the income you are entitled to receive from various sources.

2) **To know how much you have spent and what you spent on**

Some people spend money but unable to be accountable for the spending. They may not be able to explain how they spend there money. Some people may spend some amount of money and receive a balance from a vendor. They may not know where they keep the balance. If records are kept for the spending, you will be able to know whether you are having some balances somewhere or not. Some of the disadvantages of not keeping record of personal finance are as follows:

Some people always forgot money in the pockets of their cloths and washed the money along with the cloths. This is a waste of money.

Some forgot money in the pockets of their cloths and gave the cloths out for laundry. This is a waste of money.

The solution to the above disadvantages is the keeping of records of personal finance. If records are kept frequently, you will know where each amount of your money is.

1.2.2. Types of Record Keeping

The following are the some necessary records that should be kept by every individual.

1) Cash Book

2) Income and expenditure Accounts

3) Statement of Financial Position

1.2.2.1   Cash Book

Cash book is a book that is used to record cash received, cash spent, cash lodged in a bank account and cash withdrawn from the bank. You can also use your cash book to record the movement of your cash as a business entity does.

Cash book contains two sides; both debit and credit sides. Debit side is used to record cash that comes in while credit side is used to record cash that goes out.

The cash book can be classified into two. They are:
- one column cash book
- two column cash book.

One column cash book contains only cash transaction on both debit and credit sides while two columns cash book contains both cash and bank transaction on both debit and credit sides. The common type out of the two is two column cash book because many individual keep bank account.

The end result of preparing the cash book is to ascertain the cash and bank balances at the end of each month.

Note:

All transactions that occur in each month should be posted to the respective month in which they occur. For example all transactions that occur in January, 2015 should be posted to cash book for the month of January, 2015.

Example 1

Mr. Benjin is an engineer. He works with a construction company. The following are his transactions for the month of January and February, 2015.

Income:

His salary of $5,000 was paid into his bank account on January 24, 2015.

He received transport allowance $ 250 by cash on January 24, 2015.

A dividend of $100 was deposited into his bank account on January 28, 2015.

A friend that borrowed money from him paid into his bank accounts on February 5, 2015. The amount was $700.

Expenditure/out flow of cash

He bought food stuff worth $500 on January 29, 2015, by check.

He withdrew $1,200 in his bank account on January 30, 2015.

He paid for electricity bill of $300 in February 5, 2015 by check.

He paid for water bill costing $100 in February 5, 2015 by check.

He incurred $140 on consumption of fuel in January 26, 2015. He paid by check.

He deposited $1,300 to his bank account on February 6, 2015.

Benjin's cash book can be prepared from the above information.

Benjin's cash book for the month of January, 2015

Date	Particulars	Debit Side		Credit Side	
		Cash	Bank	Cash	Bank
		$	$	$	$
24	Salary		5,000		
24	Transport allowance	250			
26	Fuel				140
28	Dividend		100		
29	Food stuff				500
30	Cash withdrawn	1,200			1,200
	Balance c/d			1,450	3,260
	Total	1,450	5,100	1,450	5,100
	Balance b/d			1,450	3,260

NOTE:

It can be clearly seen that $1,200 withdrawn from bank was credited to bank column and debited to cash column.

The cash and bank balance brought forward to the following month (February,2015) are $1,450 and $3,260 respectively.

Benjin's cash book for the month of February, 2015

		Debit Side		Credit Side	
Date	Particulars	Cash	Bank	Cash	Bank
		$	$	$	$
1	Balance b/f	1,450	3,260		
5	Friend		700		
5	Electricity bill				300
5	Water bill				100
6	Deposit		1,300	1,300	
	Balance c/d			150	4,860
	Total	1,450	5,260	1,450	5,260
	Balance b/d			150	4,860

NOTE:

The cash that Benjin is having in hand as at February 6, 2015 is $150 and the bank balance at the same date is $4,860.

1.2.2.2. Income and Expenditure Account

This account shows how you earn your income and how you utilize it. It has two opposite sides called debit side and credit side. It is used to determine the amount of surplus or deficit you have at the end of each month. If the total amount of income you realized at the end of the month is higher than the total amount you spent, you will have surplus but if the total of your expenditure at the end of the month is higher than the amount you realized as income at the end of the month, then you will have deficit.

The expenditure will be recorded on the debit side while income will be recorded on the credit side.

NOTE:

The recording of income and expenditure is different from the recording of cash book because, it involves recording of both cash transaction and non- cash transaction. This is called accrual basis in accounting.

1.2.2.3 Statement of Financial Position

Your personal net worth is the best way to determine what you worth and where you are in finance. Your net worth is calculated by deducting your liability (what you owe) from your assets (what you own). Statement of personal financial position shows all the assets you have and the liability you incurred as at a particular period. The components of statement of financial position are assets and liabilities.

Assets are those properties you have which cannot be consumed within a period less than a year. The following are various categories of assets:

- Automobile value (the resale value of your car)
- Home value (the resale value of your home)
- Your computers (the resale value of your computers)
- The amount of money owed you
- Your investment
- Your cash balance and bank balance

- Credit card balance (positive figure)
- Personal property (the resale value of your jewelry, etc)

Liability is the money you owed people.

The following are various categories of liabilities:

- Cash borrowed
- Services you enjoyed but not yet paid for(accrual)
- Car loans
- Students loans
- Credit card balance (negative figure)
- Remaining mortgage balances

The difference between your assets and your liabilities is your **net worth**. You begin to increase your net worth by reducing your liability and increasing your assets. You must endeavor to calculate your net worth often in order to know what you worth.

Here is an example of a format for the preparation of statement of financial position.

Statement of personal financial position as at 31st December, 2014.

Assets	$	$	$
Automobile value		xx	
Home value		xx	
Investments		xx	
Personal property		xx	
		xx	

Money owed you	xx	
Cash balance	xx	
Bank balance	xx	
Credit card balance(+)	<u>xx</u>	
	<u>xx</u>	
Total Assets	xx	xx
Liabilities		
cash borrowed	xx	
Accrual	xx	
Credit card balance(-)	<u>xx</u>	
	xx	
Car loans	xx	
Students loans	xx	
Mortgage balances	<u>xx</u>	
Less Total Liabilities	xx	<u>xx</u>
Net worth		xx

CHAPTER TWO

SAVINGS

WHY DO YOU NEED TO SAVE MONEY?

What is your belief for saving money? Some people accept that they do not need to spare cash since they have enough to spend before the next earnings/salaries are paid. You may be asking yourself why is it necessary to save money since you have access to credit facility. In order to prove all these perceptions wrong, I sat down and put into written why you need to save money. The following are 5 important reasons you need to save money:

Save for Emergency Funds

You need to save for emergency funds. Some urgent financial needs such as repair of your car, payment for hospital bills and payment for all other unforeseen circumstances may occur. If you don't have required amount of money in your bank accounts to take care of all these situations, you may suffer unnecessarily. You need a continuous savings in order to build up emergency funds in addition to other insurance schemes you might have engaged in. It is never too late to start setting aside a percentage of your earnings or salary every month for the emergency funds. You can be saving 20% of your earnings or salary every month for these funds. If your monthly income is $800, your emergency fund will be 20% ×$800 = $160, It means that you have to save $160 each month.

Save for Old Age
You need to save for the time you will not be able to expend energy to generate income. When you become old, you will be weak and you will not be able to work well as you used to do when you were younger. Save now and save your future as well as that of your family.

Save to Gain the Benefit of Cash Purchasing

There are some benefits of cash purchasing such as cash discount and other allowances. If you purchase by cash you stand a better chance of gaining than to purchase on credit. There is what is called cash discount. It means that if you purchase goods by cash, the cost of the goods will be reduced. This means that you have to pay less for the goods. For example, if the cost of the goods is $300 and a discount allowed of 5% is given for cash purchases. The cash discount will be 5% ×$300 = $15. You will eventually pay $285 instead of $300 for the goods. If you can save your money in order to purchase by cash, you will gain this cash discount in many circumstances.

Save for Sinking Fund

A sinking fund is a stream of equal savings you made for the purpose of acquiring property or fixed assets in the future. The assets can be houses, cars and other luxuries. You have to set aside the cash meant for the purchase of these assets.

Application of Annuity to Personal Decision

The following can be used as an example to explain sinking fund.

ILLUSTRATION 1

Mr. Joe needs to provide $50,000 to replace his machine in 5 years time, in order to provide this amount he decides to set aside equal amount annually, out of his salary. This amount is kept in savings account that yield 20% interest per annum. Find this amount, and the sinking fund schedule.

SOLUTION

The calculation of each amount that will be kept aside annually to meet this need is:

$$FV = \frac{A\,[(1+r)^n - 1)]}{r}$$

$50,000 = \dfrac{A\,[(1+0.2)^5 - 1)]}{0.2}$

$50,000 \times 0.2 = A(1.2)^5 - 1$

$10,000 \qquad = A(2.4883 - 1)$

$10,000 \qquad = A \times 1.4883$

$\dfrac{\$10,000}{1.4883} \qquad = A$

$6,719 = A$

The amount that will be kept aside annually is $6,719

Sinking Fund Schedule:

Years	a Balance b/f	b Interest $	c Sinking Fund $	a+b+c Balance c/d $
1			6,719.00	6,719.00
2	6,719.00	1,343.80	6,719.00	14,781.80
3	14,781.80	2,956.36	6,719.00	24,457.16
4	24,457.16	4,891.43	6,719.00	36,067.59
5	36,067.59	7,213.52	6,719.00	50,000.11

The sinking fund for each year is $6,719

Save to Add Value to Your Money

When you save $1 in a bank account today, you will be having an amount higher than $1 tomorrow. This is what is called time value of money. The interest will be added to your savings in the bank. Your money in the bank will be increased by the addition of the interest. If you cultivate the habit of savings, you will add value to your money.

CHAPTER THREE

RETIREMENT PLANNING

Retirement is inevitable as death is inevitable to every human being. You cannot work through out your life span. There will be a time in which your energy and strength will be dwindled. At this stage of life, you will not be able to expend energy as you used to. You have no option than to retire from work. The period in which you will not be able to work is referred to as period retirement.

Even, if all of us are willing to retire comfortably, the complexity involved in retirement planning can be discouraging and intimidating. However, it only requires little assignment, savings and proper investments. Once you can do these you will rejoice at the end.

Why Retirement Planning?

We have to know the reasons for retirement planning before we discuss on other processes involved in retirement planning. The reasons for retirement planning will stimulate us to ensure that we absolutely plan for retirement. The following are the reasons for retirement planning:

1) Uncertainty of social security and Pension Benefits

Government is not finding it easy these days to implement social security and pension benefits. The numbers of employees that are contributing to the scheme are reducing and hence, the amount available to administer the pension is reducing. You need to plan for your own retirement if you don't want to be a victim of degrading in the scheme.

2) Private Pension plan

Private Pension Plans are the pension schemes that are being managed by corporation order than government. This is not reliable because corporations are being liquidated. Once corporation goes into bankruptcy, all your savings for building your future pension scheme go down.

How Much Would I Need?

How much you plan depends on your taste, your desired standard of living, your expenses including any medical costs and your target age of retirement.

How much you need to plan can also depend on the common old age at which people die in your community or environment. You can work toward this by preparing a sinking fund. The sinking fund has already been explained in chapter three of this book.

CHAPTER FOUR

PERSONAL BUDGETING

What is personal budgeting?

Personal Budget is a financial plan that allocates future personal income to future personal expenses, savings, and debt repayment. It can also be defined as a future estimate of revenue, costs and resources. It can be monthly, quarterly and yearly.

How do I create Budget?

The following steps are involved in creating personal budget.

Step 1: What are my goals?

The first step in setting up a budget is to identify and set up your goals. You goal may be to pay a debt, to buy a house, to prepare for retirement age, to minimize the debt you graduate with, to save for car or your family. Budget may involve difficult choices but having a specific goal will simplify it.

Every financial goal you set should be a SMART goal:

S = Specific

M= Measurable

A = Achievable

R = Relevant

T = Timely

Your goals can be classified into three categories:

Short-term goal: Less than a year

Mid-term goal : one to three years

Long-term goal: More than five years

For example, assume that you want to buy a car immediately you graduate from school and you have 36 months to spend in school. You have to start saving for each month now. If the cost of the car is going to be $3,000 in three years, how much do you need to save per month in order to meet up with the cost? Rate of interest on savings is assumed to be 2% per month. Annuity or Sinking fund can be used to solve this problem.

Solution:

This is an ordinary annuity.

The amount you need to set aside at the end of each month is as calculated below:

$$FV = \frac{A\,[(1+r)^{\,n} - 1)]}{r}$$

$$\$3,000 = \frac{A\,[\,(1+0.02)^{36} - 1)\,]}{0.02}$$

$$= \frac{A[2.0398 - 1]}{0.02}$$

$$\frac{\$3,000}{1} = \frac{1.0398A}{0.02}$$

$$1.0398A = 3,000 \times 0.02$$

$$A = \underline{60}$$

1.0398

A   = $57.70

You need to set aside $57.70 per month in order to meet up with the cost of the car.

Where:

FV is the future value of the ordinary annuity.

A is the equal amount to be paying at the end of each period.

r is the rate of compound interest.

n is the number of years of the payment or receipt.

PV is the present value of the ordinary annuity.

NOTE:

Take a look at the above goals. You will discover that it complies with SMART goal:

S = Specific

M= Measurable

A = Achievable

R = Relevant

T = Timely

Step 2: Where is my money coming from?

If you want your goals to be achievable, you must have reliable source or sources of income. Is your money coming from work? Is your money coming from investment? Is your money coming from student loan? Is your money coming from your parents? Is your money coming from scholarship? In a nutshell, you must have reliable sources and amount of income.

Step 3: Where is your money going?

You need to know where your money is going before you can prepare a budget. Check your bank account to know how you have been spending your money. Check how much you spent out of the cash you are holding. If you want to track the accurate records of your spending, ensure to record your expenditure on a daily basis.

Use a spread sheet to track and categorize your expenses for a month.
It is necessary to classify your expenses into 3 categories:

Fixed expenses: These include expenses such as rent, phone bill, etc that are fixed for each month. You must definitely incur these expenses.

Variable expenses: These expenses vary and not stable. They include gas, food, fuel, cloths etc. They are necessities.

Wants: These are non-essential expenses such as chips for refreshment, latest movie etc.

If you have a monthly saving goal and you include the savings as part of your spending (cash out flow), it will be easier for you to meet up with the goal if you have added it to your budget.

It will be easier to prioritize your expenses if you classified your expenditure into 3 categories as mentioned above.

Expenses will be arranged according to the order of importance and necessity. By doing this, the least important expenses can be removed in order to balance your budge (step 5).

Step 4: Make Summation and Deduction

Compare your income and expenses by deducting the expenses from your income. Does the difference between your income and expenses give you a surplus or deficit. If you get surplus as the result, you are on the right side and you can invest in your future but if your result is deficit, read step 5 below.

My Monthly Budget

Sources of Income	$
Work	500
Parents	300
Scholarship	250
Available funds/money	1050

Monthly Expenses
Necessity

Phone bill	80
Rent	200
Car Insurance	40
Groceries	250
Gas	80
Wants	
Cloths	60
Latest movie	25
Tourism	30
Total monthly expenses	<u>765</u>
Difference	**285**

The available fund minus total monthly expense is $285. This is a budget surplus.

Where you prepare your budget and you arrive at a budget deficit, you need to make some adjustments to the expenses in order to arrive at a balance figure. This will be discussed in Step 5.

Step 5: Make Adjustment if needed

Where your budget is deficit, you need to make some adjustments to the expenses in order to arrive at budget balance.

You can adjust your expenses by first cutting down expenses you incurred on wants. If after reducing the expenses on wants, you are still unable to arrive at budget balance, you can go further by reducing your variable needs expenditure in the short- term and your fixed expenditures in the long-term.

Take a look at the example below:

Smith's Monthly Budget

Sources of Income	$
Work	500
Parents	200
Scholarship	250
Available funds/money	950

Monthly Expenses	
Necessity	
Phone bill	80
Rent	200
Car Insurance	40
Groceries	280
Gas	100
Wants	
Cloths	200
Latest movie	50
Tourism	100
Total monthly expenses	1050
Difference	**-100**

The available fund minus total monthly expense is -$100. This is a budget deficit. Smith has to make some adjustments to his budget in order to arrive at budget balance.

He should first consider reducing its expenses on wants and if the reduction in expenses on wants cannot give him budget balance he should go further by reducing variable needs expenditure. It is advisable for him to reduce expenses on clothes by $100 or expenses on latest movies and tourism by $50 each.

NOTE:

Personal budget is not limited to students alone. It can be used by every individual irrespective of age.

REFERENCE

Mathematics of Finance (2015) Toye Adelaja.

www.ingramcontent.com/pod-product-compliance
Lightning Source LLC
Chambersburg PA
CBHW070759180526
45168CB00004B/1676